A CHILD'S GARDEN
of BIBLE STORIES

A Child's Garden of Bible Stories

By Arthur W. Gross
Illustrated by Marilynn Barr

Foreword

It is important for children to know Bible stories as early as possible. The stories in this book have been adapted so children will be able to read them with fluency and enjoyment. Vocabulary and sentence lengths have been taken into account and are on the level of the young reader.

Parents and teachers of children not yet able to read will find *A Child's Garden of Bible Stories* a valuable aid. The Bible stories may be read as is or used as a basis for storytelling. Biblical accuracy has been maintained in the adaptation.

The 60 stories (28 Old Testament and 32 New Testament) provide a progressive, unified account of man in his relationship to God—man in the state of innocence, man in the state of sin, and man reclaimed through faith in the atoning sacrifice of Jesus, the Son of God.

May this book delight the hearts of many young children and awaken in them a lifelong interest in the timeless truths of the Bible.

ARTHUR W. GROSS

TABLE OF CONTENTS
Old Testament

New Testament

THE OLD TESTAMENT

God Makes the World

Long, long ago there was no world. There were no birds and bees, no fields and flowers, no lakes and rivers, no sun, no moon, and no stars. There were no people either. There was nothing at all. Only God was there.

Then God made the world. He made the heavens and the earth. He made all there is out of nothing. God made the world in six days. He made a part of it each day.

Whenever God made something, He just said, "Let it be made," and it was made.

At first it was dark all around. So God said, "Let there be light." As soon as God said this, there was light. It was as bright as day.

The next day God spoke again and made the blue sky high above us, just as we see it now.

After this God told the water to gather in certain places. In this way, He made the rivers, the lakes, and the oceans. In between was the dry land.

But nothing grew on the land. There were no trees, bushes, or flowers anywhere. So God spoke and made the plants. Green grass covered the fields. Pretty flowers of many colors grew out of the ground. There were also bushes and trees of every kind. Many of the bushes had berries, and many of the trees had fruit. God gave the plants seeds so more could always grow.

God made still more. He spoke again, and at once the sky was filled with lights. He made the sun and the moon, and all the stars that twinkle at night.

The earth was beautiful now, but God made it even better. God spoke once more and made fish to swim in the waters and birds to sing in the trees. Then, on the sixth day, He spoke again. Bees flew from flower to flower. Cats and dogs played in the fields. Horses and cows walked about looking for food.

Last of all, God made the first people. God made the first man out of the dust of the earth. Then He breathed into his nose. God called the man Adam. Then God made the first woman to be a partner for the first man. The first woman was named Eve.

On the seventh day God rested. He looked at all He had made, and it was very good.

The First Home

The first people to live on earth were Adam and Eve. God wanted them to have a good home, so He planted a beautiful garden in a place called Eden.

Trees of every kind grew in this garden. Some were pretty to see, and others were good for food. Animals played on the hills. Flowers peeped out of the ground. Rivers ran through the fields.

God told Adam and Eve to take care of the garden. He said, "Be fruitful and fill the earth."

God loved Adam and Eve. He had made these first people in His very own image. They were holy. God visited them in the garden, and they were glad. He was their true Friend.

The First Sin

There were many fruit trees in the Garden of Eden. One of them grew in the middle of the garden. God spoke to Adam and Eve about this tree. He said, "You may eat the fruit of any tree in the garden, except for the tree in the middle of the garden. If you eat the fruit of this tree, you will die."

One day Adam and Eve were in the garden. The devil made himself into a snake and came to Adam and Eve in the garden.

"Did God tell you not to eat of the tree in the middle of the garden?" the devil asked Eve.

"Yes," she said. "We may eat of any

tree, except for the one in the middle of the garden. If we eat of that tree, we shall die."

"That is not true," the devil said to trick them. "You will not die. Listen to me. If you eat of the tree in the middle of the garden, you will be like God. You will be just as wise as He is."

Eve listened to the devil and was tempted. She took some fruit and ate it. Then she gave some to Adam, and he ate it.

Adam and Eve did not obey God. This was the first sin.

They were afraid because they knew that God would be very angry because of their sin. So they hid in the garden.

God came into the garden and found Adam and Eve. God punished them and sent them out of the garden. Now they would have to find a new home and work very hard for their food. They would also have pain and trouble. And they would die.

Adam and Eve were the very first people to sin. They brought sin into the world.

The Promised Savior

Adam and Eve had sinned against God. But God still loved them very much. He did not want them to be punished forever for their sin, so He gave them a wonderful promise.

He said, "When the right time comes, I will send My Son into the world. He will be born of a woman. He will become a man. He will take away your sins."

Adam and Eve heard this wonderful promise. They believed the promise. They knew that God loved them and that a Savior would be born to take away their sin.

God kept His promise. After many years God's Son was born in Bethlehem. He was named Jesus. When Jesus was a man, He lived a perfect life and never did anything wrong. Then He died on the cross to take the punishment for the sins of all people. That is why we call Jesus the Savior of the world.

The Children of Adam and Eve

Adam and Eve had many children. Their first children were Cain and Abel.

When Cain grew up, he became a farmer. When Abel grew up, he became a shepherd.

One day Cain and Abel brought gifts to God. They laid their gifts on an altar and burned them. That's how they gave their gifts to God. Abel gave his best sheep to God. Cain did not give his best crops to God.

God was pleased with Abel's gift. He was not pleased with Cain's gift, for Cain had not obeyed Him. Cain got angry and killed Abel.

God asked Cain, "Where is your brother?"

Cain answered, "I do not know. Must I take care of my brother?"

"You have sinned and killed your brother," God said to Cain. "Now the plants in your fields will not grow very well. You will not have a home. For the rest of your life you will have to go from one place to another."

Cain said, "This punishment is too hard. Whoever finds me will kill me."

So God put a mark on Cain to protect him. People who saw this mark would know they should not kill Cain.

God gave Adam and Eve another son. His name was Seth. After Seth was born, Adam lived another 800 years. He had many more sons and daughters.

Adam was almost 1,000 years old when he died.

The Flood

Many more people were born and filled the earth God had made. Some of the people loved and obeyed God. Others did not love and obey God. Soon many of the people who loved God started to sin, just like everyone else. God was very angry because of their sin. He said, "I will have to punish the people. I will send a flood to cover the earth and everyone in it."

There was one man who stayed faithful to God. His name was Noah. God wanted to save Noah and his family. He told Noah to build a large boat called an ark. He told him to put food in the ark and to fill it with animals of every kind.

When all of the animals and everyone in Noah's family were on board, God shut the door.

It began to rain. It rained for 40 days and 40 nights. Every day the water became deeper. At last the water was so deep that it covered all the hills. Everyone

and everything on the earth was destroyed. Only the people and the animals on the ark were safe.

After many days the water began to go away. At last the ground was dry. Then Noah and his family and all of the animals came off the ark. Noah thanked God for saving him and his family.

God put a rainbow in the sky and said, "This is a sign of My promise. Never again will I send a flood to cover the earth. Remember My promise every time you see a rainbow."

God blessed Noah and said, "Many children will be born in your family so the earth can be filled with people again." God's blessing came true.

Abraham's Faith in God

Noah lived to be a very old man. When he died, there were many people on earth again. Each year there were more and more. Some of these people did not love God. They made idols out of wood and stone and prayed to them.

One of the people who did love God was Abraham. He did not pray to idols. He always prayed to the one true God.

One day God said to Abraham, "I want you to move away. I want to take you to a beautiful land. When you are there, I will give you a son. I will give children and grandchildren to your son. After awhile the whole land will be filled with your children. Someday the Messiah will be born from your children's children."

Abraham obeyed God and went to the land of Canaan. His wife, Sarah, went with him. Abraham and Sarah had no children.

God said, "You do not have any children now, but look at the stars. Can you count them?"

Abraham could not count all the stars he saw in the sky.

"That's how many children you will have," God told him. "You will not be able to count them all."

Abraham believed all that God had told him. When Abraham was almost 100 years old, he still did not have any children. But Abraham believed that God would keep His promise.

Abraham and the Angels

One day when Abraham was almost 100 years old, he sat at the door of his tent. He saw three men coming near. They were the LORD and two angels. They had come to talk to Abraham.

Abraham was glad to see them. He ran to meet them and asked them to visit with him.

"I will get you something to eat," he said.

Sarah made some bread. Abraham got some meat, some butter, and some milk. He served the food to his friends. They sat down and ate.

While they ate, they said to Abraham, "Where is Sarah?"

"In the tent," answered Abraham.

The LORD said, "I will come again, and Sarah will have a son."

Sarah heard this, but she did not believe it. She laughed.

The LORD knew that Sarah had laughed. He asked, "Why did Sarah laugh? Is anything too hard for the LORD?"

God's promise came true. Soon Abraham and Sarah's son was born.

The Offering of Isaac

Abraham named his son Isaac. Isaac grew up to be a fine, big boy. Sarah and Abraham loved him very much. He was their only child.

But one day it seemed as if Isaac would be taken away from them. God came to Abraham and said, "Take your only son Isaac, whom you love, and lay him on an altar. Offer him as a sacrifice to Me."

"Oh! Must I kill Isaac?" thought Abraham. "Yes, I must obey," he said. "I will take Isaac and offer him to God."

Abraham got up early. He got some wood and a large knife. Then he called Isaac, and together they started on their way to the place where Abraham was to offer his son.

After three days they could see the place far away.

Abraham gave the wood to Isaac and told him to carry it. Abraham took the fire and the knife.

Soon Isaac said, "Father, we have fire and wood, but where is the lamb you are going to offer?"

Abraham said, "God will provide a lamb."

Abraham and Isaac walked on. When they came to the top of a hill, Abraham built an altar. He put the wood on it. Then he laid Isaac on the wood. Abraham took out his knife.

Just then God called from heaven and said, "Abraham, do not kill your son. You have shown how much you love Me. You were ready to give Isaac to Me when I asked for him." Then Abraham saw a ram in the bushes. He offered the ram as a sacrifice. How happy Abraham was! He believed more than ever that God keeps His promises.

The Ladder to Heaven

Isaac grew up and had a family. His wife's name was Rebecca. His two sons were named Jacob and Esau.

When Isaac was old, he blessed both of his sons. Jacob received the better blessing. This made Esau very angry. He said, "I will kill my brother, Jacob."

Rebecca found out how angry Esau was. She spoke with Isaac, and they decided to send Jacob away for a while. Rebecca told Jacob, "Go quickly to my brother Laban. Stay with him until it is safe to come back home."

Soon Jacob was on his way. When night came, there was no house nearby. So Jacob lay down on the ground to sleep. He put a stone under his head for a pillow.

During the night Jacob had a dream. In his dream he saw a stairway. The bottom of the stairs was on the ground, and the top reached to heaven. Angels walked up and down the stairs. God was at the very top.

God said, "I am the God of Abraham and the God of Isaac. I will give this land to you and to your children. I will be with you wherever you go."

In the morning, Jacob opened his eyes and said, "How near God is to me! This is the house of God. This is the gate to heaven."

Jacob took the stone he had used for a pillow and set it in a special place. He said, "When God takes care of me and brings me safely home again, I will build an altar at this place."

Then Jacob went on his way.

Joseph and His Dreams

Jacob became a very rich man. He had many sheep, camels, and other animals. Jacob's sons worked in the fields taking care of the animals. Joseph was one of the sons.

Jacob loved Joseph more than all the other sons. He gave him a lovely coat of many colors. The brothers did not like this. They began to hate Joseph.

One day Joseph told his brothers, "I had a dream. We were working in the field. My bundle of wheat stood up straight. Your bundles bowed to my bundle." The brothers became angry.

"Do you want us to bow to you as if you were king over us?" they said.

Then Joseph had another dream. He told his brothers, "In my dream I saw the sun, the moon, and the stars bow to me."

The brothers became very angry. Even Jacob, his father, did not like the dream.

Jacob said, "Do you want me and your mother and your brothers to bow to you?"

But Jacob kept thinking about the dreams and wondering.

Joseph Is Sold

One day Jacob said, "Joseph, your brothers are at work far from home. Go and see how they are getting along. Then come back and tell me."

Joseph put on his beautiful coat and went on his way.

The brothers saw him coming. "Look," they said. "The dreamer is coming. Let's kill him. Then we will never have to bow down to him."

Reuben, the oldest brother, heard what they said. He wanted to save Joseph. So he said, "Let's not kill Joseph. Let's put him into a deep hole."

Reuben had a plan. When no one was looking, he was going to take Joseph out of the hole and send him home.

The brothers took off Joseph's coat and put him in the hole. Reuben went away, and the brothers sat down to eat. They saw a group of men riding on camels. They were on their way to Egypt. These men bought and sold things. Sometimes they even bought and sold people.

One of the brothers said, "Let's sell Joseph to these men. They will take him far away, and we will never see him again."

The other brothers thought it was a good idea. They took Joseph out of the hole and sold him. They sold him for 20 pieces of silver money.

When Reuben came back, he looked into the hole.

"The boy is not there!" he cried. "What have you done with him? What will we tell our father?"

The brothers killed a young goat and dipped Joseph's coat in the blood. Then they took the coat to their father and said, "We found this coat. See if it is your son's coat."

Jacob said, "It is my son's coat. A wild animal surely has killed Joseph."

Now Jacob was a very sad man. He cried for his son many days.

Joseph Rules over Egypt

The men who bought Joseph took him to a land called Egypt. There they sold him to a rich man. Joseph worked for this man. He took care of the man's house and field.

For a long time things went well. Then the wife of the rich man became angry with Joseph and told lies about him. Her husband believed the lies and put Joseph into prison.

Everyone in prison liked Joseph. One night two men had dreams. God made Joseph wise. He told the men what their dreams meant.

Joseph was in prison many years. It seemed as if everyone had forgotten him. But God had not forgotten him. God had a plan for making the king remember Joseph.

One night the king had two dreams. He woke up and said, "I must find out what my dreams mean."

Someone told him that a young man in prison

could tell the meaning of dreams.

The king said, "Bring this man to me."

Joseph was brought to the king. He said, "Tell me your dreams. If God will help me, I will know what they mean."

The king told Joseph about his dreams.

Then Joseph said, "This is what the dreams mean. There will be seven years when a lot of food will grow. After that there will be seven years when only a little food will grow. This will surely come true."

"What must we do?" the king asked.

"Find a good, wise man," said Joseph. "Tell him to save all the food he can in the good years so we may eat in the bad years."

The king said, "No one is as good and wise as you are. You shall save the food, and you shall help me rule over Egypt."

The king gave Joseph his ring. He also gave him fine clothes. Everyone had to bow down to Joseph and obey him.

The Brothers Go to Egypt

Joseph saved a lot of food. The bad years came, and little food grew in the fields. But the people in Egypt had enough food to eat.

Far away in the land of Canaan, Joseph's family was very hungry.

Jacob said to his sons, "I have heard that there is food in Egypt. Go to Egypt and buy some food for us to eat."

The brothers went to Egypt and came before Joseph. They bowed down to him, just as Joseph had dreamed.

Joseph knew his brothers at once, but they did not know him. Joseph did not tell them who he was. He gave them food and sent them home.

Later the brothers went to Egypt to buy more food. Again they met Joseph and bowed to him.

This time Joseph told them who he was.

"I am Joseph, your brother," he said.

The brothers were afraid. "Joseph will punish us for selling him," they thought.

But Joseph was not angry. He kissed all the brothers to show that he forgave them.

He said, "There will be five more bad years. Bring my father to Egypt. Bring your wives and children and cattle. I will give you everything you will need."

The brothers started for home. They were very happy.

They came to their father and said, "Joseph is alive! He is a great man in Egypt. He rules over the land."

At first Jacob could not believe his sons. The news seemed too good to be true. So the brothers showed Jacob the rich presents Joseph had sent.

Then he cried, "Joseph, my son, is alive! I will go and see him before I die."

Jacob and his family went to Egypt. Jacob was so glad to see Joseph again! Joseph was glad to see his father too. Joseph took care of his father and his brothers. He gave them land and homes in the best part of Egypt.

Moses, the Leader of God's People

Jacob and his family lived in Egypt a long time. Many children and grandchildren and great-grandchildren were born to them. These people were called the Children of Israel.

At first, everyone was kind to them. But a new king came after Joseph died. The new king was not kind. He was afraid of the Children of Israel.

"What shall we do with these people?" asked the king. "They are strong, and there are many of them. They might start a war against us and take our land. We must not let them get too strong."

The cruel king made the Children of Israel work very hard. He thought this would make them weak. But God kept them strong. Then the king said that all the boy babies of the

Children of Israel should be thrown into the river and be drowned.

The mothers were afraid and very sad. One mother decided to hide her baby to keep him safe.

She put her baby boy into a basket and hid him in the tall grass near the river. The baby's sister stayed near to watch him.

After awhile, the king's daughter came to the river. The princess saw the basket. She opened it and saw the little boy. The sister thought the princess surely would throw her brother into the river. But God made the princess love the baby.

"I want to keep this baby and take care of him as my son," she said. "But first I will let a woman take care of him."

The baby's sister brought her mother to take care of him. The princess named the baby Moses.

When he grew a little older, his mother brought him to the princess. Moses lived in the palace until he was a man, but he never forgot his own people, the Children of Israel. Moses felt sad when he saw how hard they had to work.

God wanted to help His people. After many years, He did help them. He chose Moses to lead them out of Egypt and back to Canaan—the land that was their home.

The Children of Israel Leave Egypt

The Children of Israel had lived in Egypt about 400 years.

God told Moses, "It is time for My people to return to Canaan. I want you to be their leader."

The cruel king of Egypt would not let the Children of Israel go. "Who will do our hard work when they are gone?" asked the king.

Moses said, "God wants you to let my people go."

"I will not obey your God," said the king.

God sent plagues to the people of Egypt, but the king would not change his mind. Finally, God told Moses, "I will send an angel to kill the oldest son in every home. But tell the Children of Israel to kill lambs and to paint the blood of the lambs on their doors. The angel will see the blood. He will not kill anyone where there is blood on the door."

The Children of Israel did what God told them to do. In the night an angel came and killed the oldest son in every home, except in the homes of the Children of Israel.

The king called for Moses and said, "Go! Leave Egypt."

A long line of men, women, children, and cattle began to leave Egypt. They stopped when they came to the Red Sea.

Soon the king was sorry that he had let the Children of Israel go. He called out his army.

"Hurry after them and bring them back," he said.

The Children of Israel saw the army and were afraid. Moses said, "Don't be afraid. God will help us."

Then Moses held his hand over the sea, and God made a path between two walls of water. The Children of Israel walked on the path to the other side. The king's army rode fast behind them.

When the Children of Israel were safely across, God told Moses, "Hold your hand over the sea."

Moses did as he was told. The water rushed back and covered the path. It covered the king's army, and they died. Moses and the people thanked God for His loving care.

The Golden Calf

The Children of Israel walked through the desert on their way to the land of Canaan. They came to a mountain and set up camp. The mountain was called Mount Sinai.

Moses climbed up the mountain to God. God wrote the Ten Commandments on two flat pieces of stone. He gave them to Moses.

"Teach My commandments to the people," God said. "I want them to learn the commandments and know them well."

Moses stayed on the mountain for 40 days. The people got tired of waiting. It seemed as if Moses would never come back.

"Let's make some gods," the people said. "We do not know what has become of Moses."

They gathered their golden earrings and melted them. Then they made a golden calf.

The people said, "This is the god that led us out of Egypt." They prayed to the golden calf.

Moses came down the mountain carrying the Ten Commandments. He saw the people with their new god. He was so angry that he threw down the stones and broke them. He took the golden calf and destroyed it.

Moses took two new stones and brought them up to God. Once more God wrote the Ten Commandments for Moses, and Moses taught them to the people.

On the Way to Canaan

The Children of Israel traveled in the desert for 40 years.

God helped them every day. He made a cloud for them to follow in the day. He made a pillar of fire for them to follow each night. When they ran out of food from Egypt, God sent quails to eat as meat. He also gave them a kind of bread called manna.

When water was bad, God made it good. When there was no water, God made water come out of a rock.

But sometimes the people complained and did not obey God.

One day some people asked Moses, "Why are you leading us? God did not make you leader. You made yourself the leader." God punished them.

One day the people needed water. God said to Moses, "Talk to the rock. Then water will come out of it."

But Moses did not do what God said. Instead of talking to the rock, he took his staff and hit the rock. Water came rushing out.

God was angry with Moses. He said, "Because you did not believe Me, you shall not go into Canaan."

When the Children of Israel came close to Canaan, God told Moses to go to the top of a mountain where he could see the promised land. Moses died on the mountain, and God buried him.

God gave the Children of Israel a new leader. His name was Joshua. He led the people into Canaan, the land that God had promised them long ago.

Ruth

Many years later, it was very dry and there was only a little bit of food. Many people were hungry.

There was a family who lived in Bethlehem. Elimelech was the father, and Naomi was the mother. They had two sons.

"We must go to a land where there is more food," said Elimelech. So he took his family to the land of Moab.

One day Elimelech died. His sons married women of Moab. One married Orpah, and the other married Ruth.

Some time later the sons died too. Now all the women were alone.

Naomi heard that once again there was food back home. She wanted to go back to her home. Orpah and Ruth wanted to go with her and help her. But Naomi said, "It is better for you to stay here."

So Orpah said she would stay. But Ruth would not stay.

She said to Naomi, "Where you live, I will live. Your people shall be my people. Your God shall be my God."

Ruth went with Naomi. They lived together in Bethlehem.

They were very poor. Ruth went out into the fields to look for food. She came into the field of a rich man called Boaz. Boaz saw her.

"Who is this woman?" he asked.

"She is Ruth. She lives with Naomi," someone said. "She has been very kind to Naomi. She is a good woman."

Boaz made sure Ruth found food. He loved Ruth and married her. They had a son called Obed. Obed grew up and had a son called Jesse.

Jesse grew up and became the father of King David. Jesus was born from the family of David.

Samuel

A woman named Hannah lived in the land of Israel. She was sad because she had no children. She wanted a baby boy. So she prayed to God.

"Dear LORD," she said, "if You will give me a son, I will have him serve You all his life."

God gave Hannah a son. She called him Samuel. After a few years Hannah brought her son to a priest named Eli. She wanted Samuel to live with Eli and to serve God.

Eli had two sons who did not love God. Eli talked to his sons, but they would not listen. Eli did not punish them.

So God sent a message to Eli. One night Samuel was asleep when he heard someone calling him. He thought it was Eli.

He ran to Eli and said, "Here I am."

"I did not call you," Eli said. "Go and lie down again."

Three times Samuel heard someone call him. Each time he went to Eli. At last Eli knew that God was calling Samuel.

Eli said, "If you hear your name again, say, 'Speak, Lord, I am listening.' "

God called Samuel again. This time He spoke to Samuel. God said, "I will punish Eli and his sons. The sons do as they please, and Eli does not stop them."

The next morning Samuel told Eli what God said.

Soon after this there was a war. Both sons of Eli were killed in battle.

A man from the battlefield ran to Eli and told him that his sons were dead. When Eli heard the bad news, he fell off his chair, broke his neck, and died.

David, the Shepherd Boy

Samuel grew up to be God's prophet.

Saul was the king of Israel, but he was not a good king. He did not obey God.

So God said to Samuel, "Go to Bethlehem to the home of Jesse. I will make one of Jesse's sons a king in the place of Saul."

Samuel went to Bethlehem. He came to the house of Jesse. He looked at all of Jesse's sons and asked for the youngest son, David. David was a shepherd boy. When Samuel met him, he poured some oil on David's head. This meant he would be king after Saul.

King Saul's army went to war against the Philistines. The Philistines had a giant named Goliath. Every day he made fun of the Children of Israel and of their God.

Goliath said, "Send one of your men to fight with me. If he wins, we will be your slaves. If I win, you must be our slaves."

The army was afraid because the giant was big and strong.

Three of David's brothers were soldiers in King Saul's army. One day David brought food to his brothers. He heard what the giant said.

David told King Saul that he would fight Goliath. He took his sling and five smooth stones. Then he went out to fight the giant.

Goliath saw that David was just a boy. He laughed and said, "Do you think I am a dog that can be beaten with sticks?"

David said, "God is on my side. He will help me."

Then David put a stone into his sling and threw it at the giant. The stone sank into his forehead. The giant fell down. David took Goliath's sword and cut off his head. When the Philistines saw that Goliath was dead, they ran away. Saul's men ran after them and defeated them.

David and Absalom

After King Saul died, God made David king.

David had a son called Absalom. David loved Absalom very much, but Absalom did many wrong things. He wanted to be king in the place of his father.

He thought of a plan to get rid of his father and make himself king. Every morning he went to the gate of the palace. There he met the people who came to see the king. Absalom bowed to them and spoke kindly to them. He took their hands and kissed them.

He said, "My father will not be fair with you, but if I were king, I would be good to you."

This made the people love Absalom and turn against King David.

One day Absalom gathered his friends at a place called Hebron. They began to shout, "Absalom is king!"

They went to Jerusalem to kill King David. Someone told David that Absalom was coming with an army.

"Let us flee from Absalom!" David cried.

Absalom came to Jerusalem and made himself king.

Soon after this David gathered his soldiers. He sent them into battle against the army of his son.

He said to his men, "Do not hurt my son Absalom."

The two armies met in a forest. Absalom's army lost the battle. Absalom and his men ran away. Absalom's mule ran under a tree with low branches. His hair got caught in the branches. His mule ran away and left him hanging on the tree. A soldier from the army of David came along. He saw Absalom and killed him.

Soon David heard that his son had been killed. He cried, "O my son Absalom! I wish I could have died for you. O Absalom! My son, my son!"

Solomon Builds God's Temple

When David died, his son Solomon was made king.

Solomon prayed to God for help. He said, "O Lord, You have made me king. Please make me a good and wise king. Help me know what is good and what is bad, so I will be a good king for You."

Solomon's prayer was pleasing to God. He said, "I will make you wise. I will make you rich too. If you love and honor Me, I will give you a long life also." God gave Solomon more wisdom than anyone else had ever had or would ever have.

Soon after he was made king, Solomon began to build a beautiful temple for the Lord. It was made of the best wood and stone and had gold on the walls. It took seven years to build the temple.

Solomon built the temple because he loved God. When it was finished, thousands of people came to worship.

Elijah and the King

Over the years, the land of Israel had some very bad kings who did not love or obey God. Ahab was one of these kings.

He prayed to a false god called Baal. Many other people also prayed to this god. Ahab hated everyone who prayed to the true God.

Elijah was a prophet of God. He came to the king and said, "Because you pray to a false god, there will be no rain."

For three years there was no rain. The people had little food and water. Ahab was angry. He thought Elijah had caused the trouble. He tried to kill Elijah.

God said to Elijah, "Hide by the brook and drink the water. I will send birds every morning and evening.

They will bring bread and meat."

Elijah lived by the brook for awhile. Then the brook dried up. So God helped Elijah another way.

He said, "I have told a woman to take care of you. Go to her."

Elijah came to the woman and said, "Please, give me water to drink." She gave him some water.

Then Elijah said, "Please, give me some bread."

"I have only a little bit of food left for my son and me to eat," said the woman, "When it is gone, we will have to go hungry and die."

Elijah said, "Do as I tell you. God has promised that you will always have food."

The woman believed the promise of God. She took Elijah into her home and gave him food. God provided food for Elijah, the woman, and her son every day.

Elijah and the Prophets of Baal

King Ahab wanted to kill Elijah, but Elijah was not afraid.

He went to Mount Carmel and spoke to the people. He said, "Some of you believe in my God, and some of you believe in Baal. Let us find out which one is the true God. Then let us all believe in Him."

He told them, "Get two bulls. You kill one of them, and lay the meat on an altar. I will kill the other and lay the meat on an altar. Then you will pray to your god, and I will pray to my God. We will see which of the two sends fire from heaven to burn up the meat. The one who can send fire will be our God. We all will believe in Him."

The people said, "Your plan is a good one. We will follow it."

The prophets of Baal put the meat of their bull on

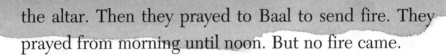

the altar. Then they prayed to Baal to send fire. They prayed from morning until noon. But no fire came.

Elijah put the meat of his bull on an altar. He told some men to pour water on the meat, on the wood, and on the altar. He also told them to fill the ditch around the altar with water.

Elijah prayed to God and said, "O, LORD, make us all know today that You are the only true God."

Then the fire of the Lord came down from heaven. It burned the meat, the wood, and the stones of the altar. It also dried the water in the ditch.

When the people saw this, they cried, "The LORD is God! The LORD is God!"

Soon the sky became dark, and there was a great rain.

Naaman and Elisha

An important and rich man was very sick. His name was Naaman. He lived near the land of Canaan.

Naaman tried many times to get well, but in his land no one could help him.

A slave girl worked in Naaman's house. She had come from the land of Israel. She wanted to help her master.

"If only my master would go to my land," said the girl. "There is a man of God there who can help him."

She was talking about the prophet Elisha. Naaman went to see Elisha.

Elisha said, "Go and wash in the Jordan River seven times. Then you will be well."

At first Naaman did not want to do this. He did not think it would help him. He said, "The rivers at home are better than all the rivers here. Couldn't I wash in them and get well?"

Then his servants said, "Master, the prophet has told you to do an easy thing. An easy thing can help you as well as a hard thing."

Naaman went to the river and washed himself seven times. Then his sickness was gone. God had made him well. Now Naaman knew that God was the one true God.

He wanted to pay Elisha for helping him. He wanted to give him gold, and silver, and fine clothes. But Elisha knew that he had not helped Naaman. It was God who had done it all.

Three Men in a Furnace

Far from the land of Israel there lived a wicked king. He prayed to a false god, an idol. The idol was made of gold, and it was very, very tall. The king wanted all of his people to pray to the idol.

One day the king called his important men together. They went to the place where the idol stood.

One of the king's men called out, "O people, when you hear the sound of music, you must bow down and pray to this god. If you do not bow down, you will be put into a furnace and burned."

Every time music played, the people bowed down and prayed to the idol. But there were three men from the land of Israel who believed in God. They did not pray to the idol.

Some friends of the king saw that they did not pray to the idol. They went to the king and said, "O king, there are three men from the land of Israel who do not obey you. They do not bow down."

The king came to the three men and said, "If you do not pray to my god, you will be put into a hot furnace. Do you think your God can save you from the fire? Who is your God?"

"Our God is able to save us," they answered. "But we would not pray to your idol even if our God would let us burn."

The king was very angry. He said to his men, "Make the fire seven times hotter." He commanded soldiers to tie up the three men and throw them into the furnace. The fire was so hot that it killed the soldiers who threw the three men into the furnace.

The king looked into the furnace and saw four men in the furnace. They were walking about in the fire and singing.

The king said in great surprise, "Didn't we put three men into the fire? Now I see four. They are not hurt. One of the four is like the son of the gods."

Now the king knew that God had saved the three men in a wonderful way. He went to the door of the furnace and called to them.

"You are servants of the Most High God. Come out," said the king.

Everyone saw that the three men were not hurt at all. Even their clothes did not smell like fire.

The king said to them, "Your God saved you because you believed in Him. There is no other God who can save like your God."

Daniel and the Lions

Daniel believed in the one true God. He prayed to God every morning, noon, and evening.

Daniel had been born in the land of Israel, but now he was living in a strange land far away.

The king of this land saw how faithful Daniel was. He chose Daniel to help him rule over the land.

Other important leaders were jealous of Daniel. "We must get Daniel into trouble with the king," they thought.

They came to the king and said, "O king, we think you should make a new law that all people must pray to you alone. Whoever prays to anyone else will be put into a den of hungry lions." The king agreed and made the law known to everyone.

The enemies of Daniel knew that he would not obey this law. They watched Daniel. They saw that he still prayed to God three times a day.

They ran to the king and told him, "Daniel does not obey your law. You must throw him to the lions."

When the king heard this, he was sorry that he had made such a foolish law. But he was not allowed to change it. So Daniel was put into a den with hungry lions.

The king got up early the next morning to check on Daniel. He called out, "O Daniel, is your God able to save you from the lions?"

Daniel answered, "My God sent His angel to shut the mouths of the lions. They did not hurt me."

The king was glad. He told his servants to take Daniel out of the den.

The king said, "The God of Daniel is the only true God."

The New Testament

The Birth of John the Baptist

A short time before Jesus was born, there lived a priest named Zechariah. His wife's name was Elizabeth. Zechariah and Elizabeth were very old, and they had no children.

One day a wonderful thing happened. While Zechariah was at work in the temple, an angel suddenly stood before him. Zechariah was afraid.

"Do not be afraid," said the angel. "God has heard you pray. He will give you a son. You shall call your son John. John will be great in the sight of the Lord. He will prepare people for the coming of the Lord."

Zechariah did not believe the angel. So the angel said, "I have been sent by God. Because you did not believe me, you will not be able to speak until your son is born."

Zechariah tried to speak, but he had been silenced.

When the time was right, Zechariah and Elizabeth had a son. Their friends came to see them. They thought the baby should be called Zechariah, like his father.

But Elizabeth said, "No. He shall be called John."

They asked Zechariah what the name should be. He wrote the name John on a tablet. At once, Zechariah could speak again.

He called out, "His name is John."

"Wonderful things are happening," the friends said to one another. "John will surely be a great man."

A Message from God

It was almost time for Jesus to be born.

A young woman named Mary lived in a town called Nazareth. She was not married, but she had promised to become the wife of a man named Joseph.

One day an angel came to see Mary. She was afraid.

"Do not be afraid," said the angel. "The Lord is with you, and He will give you a great blessing. He will make you the mother of His Son, Jesus. Jesus will be King over God's people. His kingdom will never end."

Mary was very happy. She said, "I want to be the mother of Jesus. I want to obey God in all things."

Mary went to visit her cousin Elizabeth. When the two happy women met, Mary sang a beautiful song. She thanked God for the Savior who would soon be born.

Mary stayed with Elizabeth for three months. Then she went back to Nazareth.

The First Christmas

It was time for Jesus to be born. One day Joseph came to Mary and said, "The king wants to know how many people live in his lands. He wants everyone to be counted. Everyone must have his name written into the king's books. We must go to Bethlehem where my family was born. God wants us to obey the king. So we will go."

Soon Mary and Joseph were on their way to Bethlehem. Many others came to Bethlehem too. When Mary and Joseph arrived, they wanted to find a place to rest. But Bethlehem was full of people. It was hard to find a place to stay.

Mary and Joseph looked everywhere for a place to stay. But there was no room to be found in Bethlehem. At last Mary and Joseph found a stable. That night, in the stable, Jesus was born.

Mary wrapped baby Jesus in cloths and laid Him in a manger.

Jesus, the Son of God, had come to earth. God sent Jesus because He loved the people of the world so much. One day Jesus would save the people of the world from their sin.

Shepherds Find the Savior

On the night when Jesus was born, shepherds were watching their sheep in a field near Bethlehem. It was quiet and dark.

Suddenly a bright light shone around them. The shepherds saw an angel in the light and were afraid.

"Do not be afraid," said the angel. "I bring you good news. The news is for all people. Jesus the Savior is born. You will find Him in Bethlehem in a stable."

Suddenly the sky was filled with thousands of angels.

They sang, "Glory to God in the highest; peace on earth; good will to men."

The angels left and went back to heaven. It was dark and quiet again.

"Let us go to Bethlehem and find Jesus our Savior," the shepherds said to one another.

They went to Bethlehem. They found the stable, and in the stable they found Jesus. The shepherds thanked God because He had sent the Savior into the world.

Then they went back to their field. On their way, they told everyone they saw that Jesus had come into the world.

The Star of the King

About the time Jesus was born, God put a new star into the sky. Some Wise Men who lived far away in the East saw the star.

They discovered that the new star meant a new king had been born. They left to find the king.

They rode many days. At last they came to Jerusalem.

The Wise Men asked, "Where is the new king? We have seen His star in the east. We have come to worship Him."

A wicked king named Herod lived in Jerusalem. When Herod heard this, he was angry.

"Does someone want to be king in my place?" Herod said to himself. "I will not let anyone take my place. I will kill this new king."

Herod asked some teachers where the new king was to be born.

"In Bethlehem," they said.

Then Herod told the Wise Men, "Go and find the Child. When you have found Him, come and tell me where He is. I want to worship Him also." This was not true. Herod really wanted to kill Jesus.

The Wise Men went on to Bethlehem. The star led them to the house where Jesus was.

The Wise Men bowed down and worshiped Jesus. They gave Him gold and other rich gifts.

Now the Wise Men were ready to go home.

In a dream God told them, "Do not go back to Herod." The Wise Men left and went home another way.

The Flight to Egypt

King Herod waited for the Wise Men to come back. When they did not come back, he planned another way to kill the new king. He told his soldiers to kill all the boy babies in Bethlehem.

An angel of the Lord came to Joseph at night and said, "King Herod will try to kill Jesus. Take the Child and His mother and go to Egypt. Stay there until I tell you to come back."

Joseph told Mary what the angel had said. They left quickly. Soon they were on their way to Egypt.

Herod's men went to Bethlehem. They went from house to house. They killed many boy babies, but not Jesus. He was safe and far away.

After awhile, King Herod died. An angel of the Lord came to Joseph and said, "Take the Child and His mother back to your own town. The king who wanted to kill Jesus is dead."

So Mary and Joseph and Jesus went back to live in Nazareth.

Jesus in the Temple

Jesus grew up just like the other children. He played with the boys and girls who lived near His home. He helped His father and mother when there was work to do. He studied His lessons. He was kind to everyone. He grew and grew.

Every year Mary and Joseph went to Jerusalem. They went with many other people to pray to God in the temple.

When Jesus was 12 years old, Mary and Joseph took Him along to Jerusalem. They stayed there several days. Then they started for home.

Mary and Joseph walked along the road with many others. They thought Jesus was somewhere in the crowd on the road.

They traveled for a day and began to look for Jesus. They looked along the road. They looked among their friends. They looked in the streets of Jerusalem, but they could not find Him. After three days they went back to the temple. There they found Jesus talking with some teachers about God's Word. Sometimes Jesus listened to the teachers, and sometimes He asked them questions.

"How wise He is!" thought the teachers. "How well He knows God's Word!"

Mary said, "Son, why did You stay behind? Your father and I looked for You a long time. We thought we would never find You."

Jesus said to His mother, "Why did you look for Me so long? Didn't you know that I would be in My Father's house?"

Then Jesus went back home with Mary and Joseph. He obeyed Mary and Joseph. Everyone who knew Jesus loved Him.

Jesus at a Wedding

One day there was a wedding in a small town called Cana. Mary and Jesus came to the wedding.

After the wedding there was a big party. The people ate a good dinner and drank fine wine. Everyone was happy.

But after awhile there was no more wine. Mary went to Jesus. She said, "They have no more wine."

"Leave everything to Me," Jesus said. "I will help when the right time comes."

Mary was sure that Jesus would help.

She went to the servants and said, "Be sure to do what Jesus tells you."

Jesus told the servants to fill six large waterpots with water. The servants did as they were told. Then Jesus said, "Take some of it to the chief servant."

When the chief servant tasted it, he found that it was not water anymore. It was wine. "This is the best wine we have had," said the chief servant.

Jesus had changed water into wine. This was the first miracle Jesus did. His friends believed He was the Son of God.

The Wonderful Catch of Fish

One day Jesus was on the shore of the Sea of Galilee. Many people came to see Him and hear Him speak.

Jesus saw two boats that belonged to some fishermen. The fishermen were washing their nets. One of the boats belonged to a man named Peter. Jesus stepped into his boat. He sat down and started to teach the people on the shore.

When Jesus had finished teaching, He said to Peter, "Take your boat out to the deep water, and throw out your net to catch some fish."

Peter said, "Master, we worked hard all night and caught nothing. But because You say so, I will let down my net."

Peter let the net down into the deep water. Soon it was filled with fish. The net began to tear. Some men in another boat had to come and help pull in the net. There were so many fish that they filled two boats. The boats began to sink.

Peter knew that Jesus had filled his net with fish. He fell on his knees in front of Jesus and said, "Leave me, Lord, for I am a sinful man."

But Jesus said, "Fear not. From now on you will be a fisher of men."

Jesus meant that Peter would teach others how to be saved. In this way he would catch people for God. Peter and his brother left their boats and their nets and followed Jesus. They wanted to be fishers of men.

Jesus and the Storm

Thousands of people came to hear Jesus teach. Others came to ask Him for help. Some wanted to learn how to get to heaven. Some were sick and wanted to be made well. Sometimes the people kept Jesus so busy that He hardly had time to eat.

After a busy day, Jesus was near the Sea of Galilee. He was tired, and He wanted to rest.

"Let us go to the other side of the lake," Jesus said to His disciples. "We must leave the people and rest awhile."

Jesus and the disciples got into a boat and started to cross the lake. Jesus was so tired that He fell asleep in the back of the boat.

Soon a storm began to blow across the lake. The sky became black. The wind blew strong. The waves got higher and higher. The boat began to fill with water.

The disciples were afraid. They thought the boat would surely sink.

They woke Jesus and said, "Master, save us!"

Jesus looked kindly at His friends. "Why are you afraid?" He asked. "Do you not know that I will always help you?"

Then Jesus spoke to the wind and the sea. He said, "Peace! Be still."

At once the wind stopped blowing, and the sea became calm.

"Who is Jesus?" asked the disciples. "Even the wind and the sea obey Him."

Jesus and a Sick Man

In the land where Jesus lived, there was a very sick man. He could not walk. No doctor could make him well. It seemed as if he would have to lie in bed all of his life.

One day Jesus came to the city in which the sick man lived. Some friends of the man decided to take him to see Jesus. They carried him on his bed to the house where Jesus was preaching.

There was a large crowd in the house. There were so many people that no one could get through the door.

The friends of the sick man carried him to the roof of the house. They tied ropes to the corners of the bed and slowly let it down through a hole in the roof.

Jesus saw that the man and his friends believed in Him. He said, "I forgive you all your sins."

Some people heard Jesus forgive the man's sins. They thought, "Jesus can't forgive sins. Only God can forgive sins."

Jesus knew what they were thinking. He said to them, "I will show you that I am God by making this sick man well. Then you will know that I have the right to forgive sins."

Jesus looked at the sick man and said, "Get up! Pick up your bed and go home."

At once the man got up and walked. He took his bed and went home. He was well and happy.

Many people saw Jesus make the sick man well. They were sure that Jesus was the Son of God. They were amazed at all He could do.

The Daughter of Jairus

A man named Jairus had a daughter who was 12 years old. The girl was very sick. She was so sick that she was dying.

Jairus loved his daughter, and he wanted to help her. Someone told Jairus that Jesus was in the city. So he went to Jesus and begged Him for help.

"Lord, my daughter is dying," said Jairus. "Please, come and help her. Then she will live."

Jesus went with Jairus. Before they even got to the house, a man came to meet them. He said to Jairus, "Your daughter is dead. Do not trouble Jesus to come to the house."

But Jesus said, "Have no fear. Only believe in Me."

Jesus and Jairus went to the house. Many friends were crying because the girl had died.

Jesus said to them, "Why do you cry? The girl is not dead. She is sleeping."

Jesus took the father, the mother, and three disciples into the house. He took the girl by the hand and said, "Little girl, I say to you, get up."

As soon as Jesus said this, the girl got up and walked. She was alive and well.

Her parents were very happy, but Jesus told the people not to tell anyone that He had brought the girl to life again.

The Young Man of Nain

One day Jesus went to a town called
Nain. His disciples and many other people
were with Him.

There was a stone wall around the town. In the wall,
there was a gate. Just as Jesus was about to go through
the gate, He saw people coming out. They were on
their way to bury a young man who had died.

The young man's mother was sad. Her husband was
already dead, and now she had to bury her only son.
The people felt sorry for the mother. Many of them
cried.

Jesus said to her, "Do not cry."

Then Jesus spoke to the dead man and said, "Young
man, I say to you, get up!"

As soon as Jesus said these words, the young man

sat up and began to speak. Jesus had made a dead man alive again!

The mother was very glad to see her son alive again. The people were amazed and praised God.

The people told others what they had seen. In this way, even people who lived far away came to know about the miracle Jesus had done.

The Captain and His Servant

Jesus was walking into a city near the Sea of Galilee. An army captain came to meet Him.

The captain said, "Lord, I have a sick servant at home, and he is in great pain."

Jesus said, "I will come and heal him."

"Lord," said the captain, "I am not worthy of having You come into my house. Besides, I know You can heal him from here. If You will say that my servant shall be well, he will be well. When I say to a soldier, 'Go,' he goes. When I say to another, 'Come,' he comes. When I say to my servant, 'Do this,' he does it."

Jesus knew that the captain had great faith. He said to the people around Him, "Truly I say to you,

I have not found anyone in all the land of Israel who had so great a faith as this captain."

Jesus said to the captain, "Go on your way. You believed that I would heal your servant. Therefore I have healed him."

The servant was healed at the same time Jesus spoke these words.

The Sick Man at the Pool

In Jerusalem there was a very wonderful pool of water. Sometimes an angel would come and stir the water and sick people would step into it. The first person that stepped into the water became well.

Buildings around the pool were filled with sick people. Everyone waited for a chance to be made well.

One day Jesus came to the pool. There He met a man who had been sick for 38 years.

Jesus said to him, "Do you want to be made well?"

The sick man said, "I have little hope of becoming well. I can hardly move myself, and I have no one to help me get into the water. Every time the water is stirred, someone else gets into the pool ahead of me."

Jesus said to the man, "Get up! Take your bed and go to your home."

Jesus had hardly spoken these words when the

man got up. He took his bed and started for home.

As the man went along the street with his bed, he met some enemies of Jesus. They said, "This is our holy day. No one should work on a holy day. It is not right for you to carry your bed."

"The one who made me well told me to carry it," said the man who had been sick.

"Who is it that told you to carry your bed?" someone asked.

The man who had been sick did not know who Jesus was. Sometime later Jesus met the man in the temple. Now the man knew that it was Jesus who had helped him.

He went to the men who hated Jesus and said, "It was Jesus who made me well."

Food for Thousands

Large numbers of people often came to Jesus. Many came to hear God's Word. Many who were sick came to be made well.

After one very busy day, Jesus said to His disciples, "Come, let us leave the people awhile. We must go somewhere to rest."

Jesus and His disciples got into a boat and crossed the Sea of Galilee. Thousands of people followed Him around the lake. Jesus looked at all the people coming. He felt sorry for them. They looked like sheep that had no shepherd.

Jesus spoke to the people and told them how to get to heaven. Then Jesus went with His disciples up into a mountain to rest, for He was very tired. But again the people followed Him.

It was getting late, and it was time for the people to eat. The disciples came to Jesus and said, "It is getting late. Send the people away so they can buy food in the nearest towns."

"They need not go away," Jesus said. "You give them something to eat."

Andrew came to Jesus and said, "There is a boy here. He has five loaves of bread and two small fishes. But how will that feed so many?"

Now Jesus told the disciples to have the people sit down. The people sat down in groups of 50 and 100. About 5,000 men and many women and children sat down on the grass.

Jesus blessed the bread and the fish. Then He broke it into many pieces, and the disciples gave it to the people to eat. Jesus made enough food to feed all the people who were there.

When everyone had eaten, Jesus told the disciples to gather the food that was left. They gathered 12 baskets full. All the people saw that Jesus had done a great miracle.

Jesus Walks on the Water

Late one night Peter and the other disciples were crossing the Sea of Galilee. Jesus was not with them. He had gone up a mountain to pray.

After awhile the wind blew across the dark waters. Strong waves splashed against the boat. Suddenly they saw someone walking across the water. The disciples were afraid.

"A ghost!" they cried.

"It is I," said Jesus. "Do not be afraid."

Then Peter said, "Lord, if it is You, tell me to come to You on the water."

Jesus said, "Come."

Peter stepped out of the boat and walked on the water toward Jesus. But when he saw a big wave coming toward him, he felt afraid. He began to sink.

"Lord, save me!" he cried.

Jesus took Peter by the hand and said, "Peter, did you suddenly think that I would let you go down?"

Jesus and Peter stepped into the boat. At once the wind stopped. Everyone in the boat said to Jesus, "Surely, You are the Son of God."

Mary and Martha

Not far from Jerusalem there was a village called Bethany. Two sisters, Mary and Martha, lived there. They were friends of Jesus. They were glad whenever He came to their home.

One day when Jesus was in Bethany, Jesus came to visit Mary and Martha. Mary sat down to listen to Jesus. Martha kept busy around the house. She cooked and baked. She swept and dusted. She did it all for Jesus.

Martha was worried. There was so much work to do, and she did not think she could do it all by herself. She wished that Mary would come and help her. But Mary did not come. She stayed with Jesus.

Martha went to Jesus and said, "Don't You care

that my sister lets me do all the work alone? Tell her to come and help me."

Jesus looked kindly at Martha and said, "Martha, you have been working very hard. But there is only one thing we really need to do, and that is to hear the Word of God. Mary has done that, and she will always remember what she has learned."

Jesus Blesses the Children

One day some mothers brought their children to Jesus. They wanted Him to put His hands on them and bless them.

When they came near to Jesus, the disciples stopped them.

"Do not trouble Jesus with your children," they said. "He is too busy to see them."

But Jesus did not want the disciples to stop the mothers from bringing their children to Him.

"Let the little children come to Me," He said. "Do not keep them away. I want to bring them into the kingdom of heaven."

Jesus took the happy children in His arms. He held them close to His heart. He put His hands on them and blessed them.

The Lost Son

Jesus loves us all very much. To show us how much God loves us, Jesus told a parable.

He said, "A man had two sons. One day the younger son said to his father, 'Give me the money you intend to give me when you die. I want it now.'

"The father gave him his share of the money. The younger son took all his money and went far away into a strange country. There he began to waste his money. He spent it on sinful pleasure. In a short time he had wasted it all. Now he could buy no food.

"The young man became very hungry. So he went to a farmer and asked for work so he could eat. The farmer sent him into the field to take care of some pigs. There the young man ate what the pigs ate.

"One day the young man thought about his father. 'My father has many men working for him,' he thought. 'They have more food than they need, while I am hungry each day. I will go to my father and tell him that I have

sinned. I will ask him to make me one of his workmen.'

"The young man started for home. His father saw him coming. The father ran down the road to meet him. He put his arms around him and kissed him.

"The son said, 'Father, I have sinned against heaven and against you. I am not worthy of being called your son. Please take me as one of your workmen.'

"But the father said to his servants, 'Bring the best clothes and put them on my son. Put a ring on his hand and shoes on his feet. Bring a fat calf and kill it, so we can have a fine dinner. Let us eat and be happy because my son who was lost has been found.'

"The servants did as they were told, and there was great joy in the house."

The Prayers of Two Men

Some people thought they were better than other people were.

"How good we are!" they thought. "God surely must love us best."

But these people were wrong. To show how wrong they were, Jesus told a parable.

He said, "Two men went into the temple to pray. One was proud; he thought he had no sins. The other felt ashamed; he knew he had many sins.

"The proud man looked up and said, 'God, I thank You that I am not like other people. I do not rob, I do not cheat, and I do not steal like the man here with me. I am fair with all people. I give much of my money to the poor.'

"The other man stood in a place where he was all alone. He hung his head in shame.

"He put his hand on his breast and said, 'God, be merciful to me, a sinner.'"

When Jesus had finished telling this story, He said, "This man had his sins forgiven instead of the other man. Those who are proud in their belief do not have their sins forgiven. Those who are sorry for their sins and believe in God have their sins forgiven."

The Good Samaritan

A man who knew the Law of God came to Jesus and asked, "What must I do to get to heaven?"

Jesus said, "What does the Law of God tell you to do?"

"Love the Lord your God with all your heart, with all your soul, and with all your mind. And love your neighbor as yourself," answered the man.

"That is right," said Jesus.

"But who is my neighbor?" asked the man.

To answer this question, Jesus told a parable.

He said, "A man was going from Jerusalem to Jericho. A band of robbers hid along the road. They beat him, robbed him, and ran away. They left him lying on the road.

"After a little while a priest came along. He saw the man lying on the ground. He noticed how much he needed help. But he passed by.

"Then a man who worked in the temple came along.

He also saw the man on the ground, but he did not help him either.

"Finally, a man from Samaria came riding down the road. He saw the man on the ground, and he felt sorry for him. He put oil and wine on his wounds and covered them with clean cloths. Then he put the man on his donkey and brought him to an inn. He stayed with him all night.

"In the morning the Samaritan went to the owner of the inn. He gave him some money and said, 'Take good care of the wounded man. If the money I gave you is not enough, I will pay you more when I come again.'"

When Jesus finished telling the story, He asked, "Which of the three do you think acted most like a neighbor to the man who was robbed?"

"The one who helped him," the man answered.

Jesus said to him, "Go and do as he did."

Ten Sick Men

Ten men were sick with a disease called leprosy. Sores covered their bodies. No doctor could help them. They had to live by themselves so other people would not catch the sickness from them.

If anyone came too near, they called out, "Unclean! Unclean!" This meant that people should stay away or they might get sick also.

One day they saw Jesus coming down the road. They called to Him from a distance and cried, "Jesus, Master, have mercy on us!"

The 10 men believed that Jesus could help them.

Jesus said, "Go and show the priests that you are well."

As they went on their way, they suddenly saw that the leprosy had left them. Jesus had made them well.

One of the men went back to Jesus. He fell down on his knees and thanked Jesus for what He had done.

Jesus said, "Didn't I help 10 men? Where are the other nine? Did only one come back to thank Me?"

Then Jesus looked at the man who thanked Him and said, "Go your way. Your faith has made you well."

Jesus and the Blind Man

One day Jesus said to His disciples, "Come, we are going to Jerusalem." Then He said something His disciples would not understand until later. He said, "When we get to Jerusalem, all that has been written will be fulfilled. People will take Me and beat Me. They will nail Me to a cross. Then I will die. But on the third day I will rise again."

On the way to Jerusalem they passed through a city called Jericho. A blind man sat by the side of the road and begged for money.

The blind man heard the noise of many people walking along the road. "Why are there so many people on the road today?" he asked.

Someone told him that Jesus was passing by. The blind man knew that Jesus could help him.

He began to call out, "Jesus, have mercy on me!" Some men told the blind man to be quiet.

But again the blind man called, "Jesus, have mercy on me!"

Jesus heard the man call. He stopped and said, "Bring the man to Me."

When the blind man stood before Him, Jesus said, "What do you want Me to do for you?"

"Lord, I want to see!" said the blind man.

"You shall see," Jesus said. "Your faith has healed you."

As soon as Jesus spoke, the blind man could see. He praised God. The people who saw the miracle praised God too.

Jesus Rides into Jerusalem

Jesus was on His way to Jerusalem to suffer and die for the sins of all people. His disciples were with Him.

When they came close to Jerusalem, Jesus told two of His disciples, "Go into the village that lies straight ahead. There you will find the colt of a donkey. Bring it to Me."

They brought the donkey to Jesus. They put Jesus on its back. Then Jesus began His ride into Jerusalem.

A great crowd of people ran out to meet Him. Some laid their coats on the road. Others cut branches from the trees and laid them along the way. Some walked in front of Jesus, and others walked behind. They sang and praised God.

They said, "Hosanna to the Son of David! Blessed is He that comes in the name of the Lord; Hosanna in the highest."

There were enemies of Jesus in the crowd. They became angry when they heard the friends of Jesus honoring Him. They called a meeting and made plans to kill Jesus.

Judas Turns against Jesus

The enemies of Jesus made a friend named Judas. He was one of Jesus' disciples. One day Judas met with the enemies of Jesus.

He said, "What will you give me if I tell you when and where to capture Jesus?"

"We will give you 30 pieces of silver," they answered.

Judas took the offer. He watched for a chance to capture Jesus. The time came right after Jesus and His disciples ate their last meal together.

On Thursday night, Jesus sent Peter and John to find a place for them to eat their Passover meal. They found a room and got the meal ready.

Jesus and His 12 disciples went to the room and sat down to eat. During the meal, Jesus said, "One of you will tell My enemies where to capture Me."

Soon Judas left the room. He went to meet the enemies of Jesus. He told them to follow him to a garden where they would find Jesus.

"Watch whom I kiss," Judas said. "That one will be Jesus."

Jesus in Gethsemane

It was late at night. Jesus left the room after supper and led His disciples to a garden named Gethsemane. Jesus left most of His disciples near the gate.

He took three of His disciples into the garden with Him and said, "Stay here while I go on to pray."

Three times Jesus went further into the garden to pray. Each time He came back, He found the disciples asleep.

Judas and a large crowd of men came into the garden carrying torches and swords. Nearer and nearer they came. Suddenly Judas stepped out of the crowd and went to Jesus. He kissed Jesus to show whom the enemies should take away.

Jesus said, "Judas, are you helping My enemies by giving Me a kiss?"

Then some soldiers crowded around Jesus to arrest Him. Peter wanted to fight for Jesus. He took his sword and cut off a man's ear, but Jesus told Peter to put his sword away. Then He healed the man's ear.

The disciples watched as the enemies led Jesus away. They became afraid and wondered if they would be arrested too.

Jesus before the Judges

The enemy soldiers took Jesus back into Jerusalem. They brought Him before the High Priest.

The High Priest asked Jesus, "Are You the Christ, the Son of God?"

"I am," answered Jesus.

The High Priest said this was a lie. He became angry and tore his clothes. He asked the enemies what they thought about Jesus.

"He is guilty and should die," they cried.

The soldiers in the crowd began to hit Jesus. They spit on Him and made fun of Him.

The High Priest could not order Jesus to be put to death. So he sent Jesus to the governor whose

name was Pilate. He was the only one who could give the order to put someone to death.

Pilate asked the enemies, "What wrong has this man done?"

They said, "He has caused trouble and turned the people against the king. He says that He is King."

So Pilate went to Jesus and asked, "Are You the King of the Jews?"

Jesus answered, "My kingdom is not of this world."

"Are you a king, then?" Pilate asked.

"Yes, I am a king," said Jesus.

Pilate said, "I find no fault with this man. I will punish Him and set Him free."

But the enemies cried, "Crucify Him!"

Pilate told his soldiers to hit Jesus. Other soldiers made a crown of thorns and pressed it onto Jesus' head. Some even spit on Him. Pilate brought Jesus before His enemies once again.

"Crucify Him! Crucify Him!" they cried.

Pilate saw that the people were angry. He let them have their way and gave the order to crucify Jesus.

Pilate washed his hands and said, "I do not want the blame for killing this man." Then the soldiers led Jesus away to crucify Him.

The Death of Jesus

Outside the city of Jerusalem was a hill called Golgotha. There the enemies of Jesus nailed Him to a cross. While Jesus was on the cross, He spoke several times.

He prayed for His enemies. He said, "Father, forgive them, for they know not what they do."

Two thieves were crucified with Jesus. One of them was sorry for his sins and believed in Jesus.

Jesus said to him, "Today you will be with Me in heaven."

Jesus looked down from the cross and saw Mary, His mother. He also saw His disciple John.

He said to his mother, "John will take care of you like a son takes care of his mother."

To John, He said, "See, this is your mother."

Jesus was very thirsty. He said, "I thirst." Some soldiers gave Him vinegar to drink.

Then Jesus said, "It is finished."

He bowed His head and died for the sins of the whole world. As soon as Jesus died, the earth shook, and large rocks split apart.

The captain of the soldiers saw this and said, "Surely this man was the Son of God."

Late in the afternoon some friends of Jesus came to the cross. They took Jesus' body down from the cross and laid it in a tomb. They closed the door of the tomb with a large stone.

Pilate sent some soldiers to guard the tomb.

The First Easter Day

Very early on the third day, God sent an angel to roll the stone away from the door of the tomb. The earth shook and the soldiers were afraid. They fell to the ground as if they were dead.

Three women came to visit Jesus' tomb. They saw that the stone had been rolled away. They looked in the tomb, but it was empty. What had happened? Jesus was not there.

Two angels in gleaming clothes appeared to the women. The angels said, "Why do you look for the living among the dead? Jesus is not here. He has risen, just like He said He would."

The women ran back to Jerusalem and told the disciples what they had seen.

Peter and John hurried to the tomb to see for themselves. The grave was empty.

Mary came back to the tomb and felt sad. Mary heard someone close by. She thought it was the man in charge of the garden.

"Sir," she said, "if you have taken Jesus away, please tell me where you have put Him."

The man said, "Mary."

Then Mary knew that it was Jesus. She turned and said, "Master!"

Jesus said, "Go and tell My disciples that I am alive again and that soon I will go to My Father in heaven."

Mary was very happy. She ran to the disciples and told them that Jesus was alive and that He had spoken to her.

Jesus Appears to His Disciples

On the evening of the first Easter Day the disciples were together in a room. They had locked the doors because they were afraid of the enemies of Jesus. All of the disciples were in the room, except the one named Thomas.

Suddenly Jesus stood among them.

"Peace be to you!" He said.

At first the disciples were afraid.

"Why are you afraid?" said Jesus. "Look at the marks the nails made in My hands and feet, and see that it is Me."

Jesus showed them His hands and feet. Now the disciples knew that it was really Jesus. They were very happy.

After a little while Jesus left them. When Thomas came back, the others said, "We have seen the Lord."

But Thomas would not believe them. "Unless I see the marks of the nails in His hands and put my finger into the marks, I will not believe that Jesus is alive," he said.

A week later the disciples were together again. This time Thomas was with them.

Suddenly Jesus was in the room. "Peace be to you!" He said.

Jesus said to Thomas, "Put your finger here, and see My hands. Do not doubt, but believe."

Now Thomas believed that it was Jesus. "My Lord and my God!" he cried.

Jesus said to him, "Thomas, because you have seen Me, you have believed. Blessed are they that have not seen and yet have believed."

Jesus Returns to Heaven

Jesus stayed on earth for 40 days after He had risen from the grave. During these days He showed Himself to His disciples many times. He wanted them to be sure He was really alive.

One day Jesus said to them, "Soon I will return to heaven. After I am gone, I want you to teach the Good News of God's love to all people."

Then Jesus took His disciples to a place called Bethany where they followed Him to the top of a small mountain.

Jesus lifted His hands and blessed His disciples. While He blessed them, He began to rise from the ground. Higher and higher He went. The disciples watched Him as He rose toward heaven. At last a cloud hid Him from their sight.

So it was that Jesus went to His home in heaven.

Suddenly the disciples saw two angels in white

clothing standing beside them. "You men of Galilee," the angels said, "why do you stand here looking up to heaven? Jesus will come again."

The disciples prayed and went back to Jerusalem. They were filled with joy, and they praised God for His great goodness toward the sinful people of the world.